THE GALACTIC WAR

PROLOGUE

When I was just a boy—young, yet already deeply aware of the world around me—my favorite space opera novels finally arrived on the big screen.

Of course, it was Star Wars.

The moment those starships roared across the screen, something stirred inside me. A strange, unshakable fascination.

It wasn't just fiction. It felt... familiar.

The Dark Side order.

The spaceships.

The rebellion.

The planets.

The alien races.

Have you ever felt that eerie sense of déjà vu? Like you were not just a spectator, but a soul remembering?

This next chapter in the saga is the story of how Fer lived through those years. Of how Eve was there too—though their paths never crossed at that time as lovers.

Are you ready for more? For a story that might change how you see reality itself?

Come along for another adventure... and don't expect to think the same way ever again.

— The Author

CHAPTER I – The War Action

"Wow. The speed of this fighter ship is vertiginous," Fer said, his voice sharp and alive through the communicator built into his helmet.

"Take it easy. You don't want to crash on your first flight, do you?" came the teasing reply from his big friend over the channel.

Fer laughed, his green eyes gleaming behind the visor.

"As if that would be the first time…"

Around them, the fleet of crusaders and fighter ships moved into formation—sleek, deadly, and ready for action.

The entrance of a new species into the Galactic Sector had thrown everything into chaos. Tensions were escalating fast.

A declaration of war felt imminent.

Of the seventy-five planets under Confederation control, Macabe had grown into the most powerful. From there, laws were dictated. From there, decisions were handed down like decrees from gods.

Representatives from every planet—ambassadors and their vast network of advisors—were summoned for an emergency council. The air was thick with dread.

The newly arrived species had been gaining influence, their promise of "help" masking their true intentions. Through chemical medications and mental implants, they began indoctrinating populations.

Some planets, seduced by their message, joined the movement—abandoning self-determinism in favor of a "more evolved" future.

Castes were formed.

A new police force emerged to enforce their "progressive" laws.

The galaxy trembled. Communication channels fell silent.

Then the Big Counselor stood, his voice echoing in the chamber of the central estate:

"We have no choice.

A declaration of war… against this newly arrived species, and all who stand with them."

The words reverberated like a death knell.

Across the chamber, delegates rose and departed—each returning to their home planets, their fleets mobilizing.

In the shadows, the Insidious Lord smiled.

His plan was working perfectly.

Chaos had come.

CHAPTER II — The Intrepid Fight Pilot

Fer lay on his bed in the cramped space he called home, deep inside the massive space complex. His thoughts swirled quietly—until the communicator screen lit up.

"Fer, have you not heard?
We need to go.
War has been declared.
Report to the flight station immediately."

Fer jumped to his feet and grabbed his uniform.

"On my way. See you there."

The sliding door hissed open, revealing a scene of frenzied urgency.

Everyone scrambled to get to their assigned positions.

Fer tried to remember where he was meant to report. A colleague spotted him and raised an arm.

"Come with me, daydreamer."

As usual, Fer was the last to join the group.

"Now that all the ladies have finally arrived," the Captain quipped, "let's hear the final instructions."

Groups formed quickly on the space deck. As orders were issued, crew members rushed off to their designated transport ships.

Fer was assigned to one of the Federation's Crusader-class vessels—his gateway to the space fighter fleet.

Passing through the corridor to his new cabin, Fer felt a strange sense of déjà vu. A graceful figure moved along the main access hallway.

He turned to get a better look, but was shoved aside in the crowded passageway.

Someone whispered nearby:

"She's one of the Confederation Councillors. We'll be returning her to her home planet."

Eve, the councillor in question, passed by. She too felt the uncanny twinge of familiarity.

Moments later, the Crusader disengaged from the central complex and began its journey.

Fer left his belongings behind and made his way to the control room, determined to witness the launch.

Ahead, through the vast curved glass of the command deck, space began to blur as the vessel accelerated to light speed.

A missionary handed the Commander a portable screen, which he read aloud:

"Take the Councillor to a safe location. Stop. Rendezvous at the Macab war assembly point. Stop."

The Commander placed a hand on the navigator's shoulder.

"Full speed to the Councillor's home planet."

Meanwhile, Fer was escorted away by security personnel. He could feel the tension rippling through the crew.

The war had begun.

CHAPTER III — Finally Into Action

The Crusader's engine was outfitted with a revolutionary system—one capable of generating antimatter by creating a controlled black hole in front of the ship.

These "holes" were not travel corridors from point A to B. Instead, they bent time itself. Within them, movement ceased and time dissolved. You left from A and arrived at A—instantly.

The vessel could now cross the entire galaxy in mere moments, achieving speeds thousands of times faster than light.

Fer understood this technology well. It was the one lesson that had ever snapped him out of a daydream.

But something felt off as they approached the planet meant to host the Ambassador.

No contact from the defensive station.

Then, from behind the Purple Planet, a hostile Crusader-class warship emerged—without warning, it fired a proton blast from its main cannons.

The Commander, ever vigilant, had already activated the ship's defenses. The blast was deflected.

Enemy fighters flooded out of the warship's bay like hornets from a nest.

Uncharacteristically, Fer was the first to respond to the call. He led the vanguard as they launched from the Crusader's gaping hangar mouth.

The sky became a tangled web of laser fire.

Fer's fighter—part of a new generation of high-speed vessels—had the edge. Enemy ships began to disintegrate under the pressure of his squad's agility and power.

"Fer, ease up!" his colleague called out.

"This is what I call speed!" Fer laughed.

A blast echoed near his fighter. He smirked.

"Another one bites the dust."

The experimental fighter's technology had delivered its surprise blow.

Soon, the enemy retreated, darting back to their mothership and vanishing into a black hole.

Cheers erupted inside the fighters and across the Crusader's bridge.

Fer pulled off a daring aerial loop, nearly colliding with the Crusader itself.

"Can you come back inside?" a voice crackled over comms.

"We're waiting for you."

CHAPTER IV — Time to Fight

The guest vessel delivered the Ambassador and her staff to the capital of the Purple Planet.

Ahead of their arrival, a pair of guard robots scouted the area to ensure safety.

On the way to her accommodation, Eve began removing her formal diplomatic attire.

"What are you doing?" asked one of her more assertive colleagues.

"No more diplomacy," Eve replied. "It's time to fight back."

She wasted no time, slipping into her pilot uniform and marching toward the war conference room.

General Tom looked up from his desk as she entered, her stride unflinching.

"What are you doing in uniform?" he demanded.

"Father," she said firmly, "my diplomatic role no longer serves any purpose.
 I'm joining my fighter unit."

Before he could respond, a blaring alarm interrupted their exchange.

A hostile warship approached the capital city—its trajectory a direct frontal attack.

"Activate all defenses," General Tom ordered the engineering crew.

Eve sprinted toward her old fighter squadron's hangar.

"Your ship's prepped and ready," said the flight assistant as she approached.

"You know me too well," she grinned. "Let's get this baby in the air."

Meanwhile, near the planet's gravitational boundary, the Confederation's Crusader remained in battle-readiness.

As the approaching enemy vessel entered anticipated space, it revealed itself to be a hologram—confirmed when a photon blast passed harmlessly through it, distorting only the projected image.

Engineers scanned the system for further surprises.

Then, from behind the blinding red star that bathed the Purple Planet in light, an immense swarm of enemy fighters emerged, raining proton blasts onto the planet's defenses.

Fighters from the planet scrambled to intercept—Eve among the first to respond.

The Crusader's squadron soon joined the fray, with Fer leading his team into the heart of the enemy formation.

The sky lit up—a kaleidoscope of flashes and lasers signifying each fallen ship.

Eve called out for backup—an enemy fighter had locked onto her.

Fer's voice came through comms:
 "Don't worry—I've got your tail."

He soared upward in a swift arc and blasted the pursuing fighter just before it could fire.

"Boom—gone!" Fer chuckled.

"Thanks—whoever you are," Eve said, breathless.

"Fer. Fer of the Federation. For your excellence." he replied with a laugh.

Once again, the elite pilot had tilted the tide.

The fighters were recalled to prepare the Crusader for its next destination: Macabe, the strategic rendezvous point for this increasingly murky war.

Eve returned to the planet, thinking:
 "Only when threatened by death do we truly feel alive."

CHAPTER V — The Confederation Strategy

From his cabin window aboard the Crusader, Fer gazed out at a vast gathering of Confederation warships—every vessel anchored at the Macabe rendezvous point.

Inside the command bridge, leaders of the democratic alliance convened to design their next moves.

"The key is knowing which planets are our allies, and how each can support the war effort," said General Tom.

The communication center reached out to all 75 habitable planets, encrypted messages sent to determine allegiances and capabilities.

Soon, the galaxy map on the main display pulsed with color—each hue denoting friend or foe.

With the strategy locked in, commanders returned to their ships with clear objectives: establish secure pathways to safeguard the Confederation's heart and its democratic governance.

Macabe became a fortress.

Space stations orbiting nearby were outfitted with high-powered proton weapons.

Other key planets—such as the Blue Planet—received similar defensive upgrades.

In response, enemy worlds launched heavy volleys of proton strikes.

City shielding failed to hold under the pressure. As the barriers collapsed, the blasts struck planetary surfaces.

No bodies remained—just vaporized echoes. Disintegration defined this galactic war.

Where once there was trade and unity, now only aggression and annihilation.

The Confederation would never be the same.

A shadow loomed over its future.

CHAPTER VI — *After the Storm Came the Bonanza*

Fer returned to the Crusader again and again, battle after battle—each time leaving behind beloved comrades.

His laughter had long since faded.

War was no longer thrilling. It was grief, repetition, loss.

"Will this madness ever end?" he wondered aloud.

Then, unexpectedly—silence.

Weapons ceased fire.

Enemy attacks halted.

The main planet's communication centers scrambled for data, desperate to decipher the sudden stand-down.

No explanations. Just retreat.

War strategists grew suspicious, ordering heightened alert levels.

Fer was assigned to a covert recon mission deep into enemy territory.

Flying low beneath detection systems, his squad conducted live surveillance—broadcast to the Crusader's bridge.

But across countless battlefield zones, the same eerie pattern emerged.

No movement. No signals. No presence.

Even enemy cruisers—once formidable—were nowhere to be found.

Fer landed in the hangar, puzzled. Something didn't add up.

"Did we win?" he asked himself. "It doesn't feel like victory."

Outside, even near the volatile Blue Planet, there was quiet.

Eve stood beside General Tom, staring into the void where once there had been cannon fire—now, only shadows.

They exchanged confused glances.

"This makes no sense. Why did they just… stop?" Eve asked.

Tom responded slowly:
"Looks like they went underground... hiding from something."

Was the war truly over?

No one knew.

CHAPTER VII - Secret Weapon

Fer arrives back on the planet aboard one of the transports.

Life here appears normal.

It's hard to believe that not long ago, he was immersed in brutal combat.

As he gazes at the iconic Confederation Councillors building, a bizarre cloud formation creeps over the city.

Reddish-grey in colour, it rolls across the sky like a vast blanket.

Strange magnetic resonance sounds confirm that it's not a natural cloud formation.

Fer isn't the only one watching—it draws everyone's eyes upward.

A wave of fear spreads as erratic agitation erupts into chaos.

Suddenly, a gust of wind surges from the cloud, carrying a mechanical voice.

At the same moment, a deep vibration causes severe head pain.

This incident strikes the entire Galactic sector simultaneously.

Just as quickly as it came, it vanishes.

Fer opens his eyes, having clenched them against the pain.

He notices a shift—people who were helping each other now seem filled with hatred.

Where once there was friendliness, now there's selfishness and a desire to harm.

Fights break out across the area.

Fer attempts to return to the spaceship, but some have set the space transports on fire.

The area has become dangerously unstable.

Bodies begin falling from tall buildings.

Fer flees toward the outskirts of the city.

Reaching a nearby mountain, he looks back.

Enemy spacecraft are landing in the building fields, soldiers disembarking and "cleansing" the surrounding zones.

Fer recognises the vessel that lands at the entrance.

The Insidious Lord, flanked by his elite group, has seized control.

A flash in Fer's mind makes the truth painfully clear: the Galaxy War is over—but the victors aren't the Democratic Confederation.

The Invaders now rule.

And no one knows what comes next.

CHAPTER VIII - Survive Another Day

Eve slowly recovers from the sound-induced trauma.

The once-friendly atmosphere is gone.

People who once showed kindness now isolate themselves, acting as though they alone matter.

Eve searches for her family, but like everyone else, they appear helpless and hopeless.

Looking for a way to ready a fighter spacecraft, she sees incoming ships filled with troops.

Robotic soldiers—agents of the new government.

They command everyone to return home and await further instructions.

The chaos is overwhelming.

Eve runs toward the secret passage beneath the Palace, which leads to the nearby mountains.

Leaving behind her entire life, she begins an anonymous journey into the surreal unknown.

Her only thought: survive another day.

CHAPTER IX - Prison Planet

With the new regime firmly established, rebellion begins to rise from various corners.

Artists, engineers, and other creative minds speak out against the oppressive new laws.

Day by day, people are arrested without trial and taken to secluded locations.

As these detention centres overflow, and control slips further, a final solution is being planned.

At the highest levels of the Confederation, the Security Ambassador requests to speak.

As his pod moves to the centre of the vast round chamber, voices swell around him.

"Comrades, we face a major security threat. Our facilities are overflowing."

He continues: "We propose using a boundary planet, outside our primary trade routes, to relocate these criminals."

A holographic projection of a solar system appears in the chamber's centre.

"The third planet from this star possesses the ideal conditions to sustain a meat-based organism," he says, pointing with a laser.

"I suggest we designate it a Prison Planet—to house current and future criminals."

A loud cheer fills the room.

The plan is accepted.

As another piece of the regime's grand design falls into place, the subversive race begins tightening its grip on the entire Galactic sector.

CHAPTER X — Caught in the Act

Unaware of the Confederation's latest moves, Fer moved quietly through the city's gates. Wrapped in a full brown mantle that concealed even his face, he continued meeting covertly with members of the rebellion.

Together, they planned to ignite a movement so large, no force could halt it.

As daylight faded, Fer approached a quiet door with a plan to propose. The silence in the area made him uneasy.

Beneath his cloak, his hand instinctively reached for the hilt of his light sword.

The door slid aside. A bearded man waited inside.

"Come in," he said, though his voice trembled slightly.

Fer caught the tension and stepped through cautiously.

Familiar faces sat around the table.

He asked bluntly, "Is everything alright?"

The bearded man subtly nodded toward Fer's sword-hand.

Fer followed his gaze—and froze. Each of his friends wore a small electronic device, locking their bodies in place.

The sliding door hissed open again. Confederation guards stepped inside and began taking the rebels, one by one, to the prison transport.

Moments later, the vehicle halted. A guard opened the reinforced door and guided the detainees into a towering Confederation facility.

They were led to isolated circular chambers, each seated in a harnessed chair.

A massive dome-shaped screen filled their view.

A fluid sensation spread through Fer's veins, followed by a high-pitched tone that stabbed at his ears.

Then—images.

Fast. Blinding. Uncontrolled.

Thoughts and memories surged wildly inside Fer's mind.

It was overwhelming. Confusing. Violent.

And then, just as suddenly—it stopped.

CHAPTER XI — A Life of Lies

Life on the blue planet Earth appeared... normal.

Wake up early. Go to work. Return to a house that would take a lifetime to repay. That alone was considered success.

Everyone had their assigned roles—quiet lives shaped by the environment's unspoken rules.

Children played in backyard gardens on sunny weekends. Picnics. Barbecues. A world at peace.

Fer was now one of them.

A wife. Children. A life that seemed to make sense.

But when he looked closer—at the cars, the homes, the seamless system—he felt something odd.

Déjà vu.

*"Why does this remind me of something else?
 Another place... another planet?"*

As his gaze reached farther, past Earth's surface and into the stars, the hidden reality began to surface.

On the shadowed side of Earth's moon stood a vast and secretive structure. Inside, strict surveillance monitored everything on the planet below.

They were the wardens of the **Prison Planet**.

The Matrix was embedded deep within every living being. Purposes and dreams implanted. Personalities designed.

Where once were engineers and artists, now existed identities shaped by invisible forces.

No rebels. No resistance.

To ensure compliance, a cunning race lived among them—observers in disguise, enforcing the Macabe Confederation's final decree.

Medications and subtle manipulations kept the population subdued.

Sleepwalkers. Locked in looped lives.

CHAPTER XII — XXI Century Recalls

In yet another crafted lifetime, Fer was no longer a rebel—he was an elite officer of the Macabe Confederation. He had become one of the very oppressors who once hunted him.

A new report reached Macabe command: a man, unimplanted and awakened, was pulling people out of the Matrix.

Fer received a mission:
Locate. Eliminate. Erase the truth.

Dressed in his dark blue uniform and white officer cap, Fer marched toward the launch hangar.

"Is everything ready?" he asked the white-clad crew.

"Yes, sir."

Fer climbed into the compact interstellar spacecraft. The hatch closed behind him.

Without sound, the ship lifted, slicing upward through Macab atmosphere.

Then—click.
A flash.
The ship vanished at hyper-speed.

Looping behind the moon and using sunlight for cloaking, Fer entered Earth's atmosphere, guided toward the Orient coordinates.

He changed into civilian clothes, blending in with the planet's population. Using a remote, he submerged his ship in a hidden lake.

A final glance at the mission monitor:
 Coordinates to find the awakened man.

Objective: Destroy all evidence of the Matrix's breach. Terminate the enlightened being.

But history unfolded differently.

Fer didn't complete the mission.

Instead, he joined the Galactic Rebellion—helped awaken countless minds, exposed the psy-control systems, and shattered the illusion.

Now:

I remain the most WANTED being in the Galaxy.

www.ingramcontent.com/pod-product-compliance
Lightning Source LLC
Chambersburg PA
CBHW071256070526
44583CB00017B/2496